My Little Book of
POEMS

Selected by REBECCA HELLER
Illustrated by FRANCES SCORE MITCHELL

A GOLDEN BOOK • New York
Western Publishing Company, Inc.
Racine, Wisconsin 53404

ACKNOWLEDGMENTS

The editor and publisher have made every effort to trace the ownership of all copyrighted material and to secure permission from copyright holders. Any errors or omissions are inadvertent, and the publisher will be pleased to make the necessary corrections in future printings. Thanks are due to the following authors, publishers, and agents for permission to use the material indicated:

Thomas Y. Crowell, Publishers, for "The Ducks" and "Snow," from THE GOLDEN FLUTE, edited by Alice Hubbard and Adeline Babbitt, copyright 1932 by Harper & Row, Publishers, Inc. Doubleday & Company, Inc., and The Society of Authors for "Singing Time," from THE FAIRY GREEN, copyright 1923 by George H. Doran Company. Elsevier-Dutton Publishing Company, Inc., for "Little Bug," from STORIES TO BEGIN ON, copyright 1940 by E. P. Dutton & Company, Inc.; renewal 1968 by Rhoda W. Bacmeister. Aileen Fisher for "Birthday Cake," from RUNNY DAYS, SUNNY DAYS, Copyright © 1958 by Aileen Fisher. Harper & Row, Publishers, Inc., for "First Snow" and "My Zipper Suit," from A POCKETFUL OF POEMS, copyright © 1957 by Marie Allen Howarth. Harper & Row, Publishers, Inc., and World's Work Ltd. for "The Park," from CRICKETY CRICKET!: THE BEST-LOVED POEMS OF JAMES S. TIPPETT, copyright 1927 by Harper & Row, Publishers, Inc.; renewal 1955 by James S. Tippett; first published in Great Britain 1975 by World's Work Ltd. Ruth W. Jackson for "Hippity Hop to Bed," from THE PETER PATTER BOOK, copyright 1918. Barbara Boyden Jordan for "Mud," from Child Life, April 1930. McGraw-Hill Book Company for "Fuzzy Wuzzy, Creepy Crawly," from HEY BUG! AND OTHER POEMS, selected by Elizabeth M. Itse, copyright © 1972 by American Heritage Press. Viking Penguin, Inc., for "Firefly," from UNDER THE TREE, copyright 1922 by B. W. Huebsch, Inc.; renewal 1950 by Ivor S. Roberts; copyright 1930 by The Viking Press, Inc.; renewal 1958 by Ivor S. Roberts and The Viking Press, Inc. Western Publishing Company, Inc., for "Silly Puppy," from A GOLDEN BEDTIME BOOK, copyright ©1955 by Western Publishing Company, Inc.

Singing-time

I wake in the morning early
And always, the very first thing,
I poke out my head and I sit up in bed
And I sing and I sing and I sing.

Rose Fyleman

Mud

Mud is very nice to feel
All squishy-squash between the toes!
I'd rather wade in wiggly mud
Than smell a yellow rose.

Nobody else but the rosebush knows
How nice mud feels
Between the toes.

Polly Chase Boyden

Little Bug

A weeny little bug
Goes climbing up the grass.
What a lot of tiny little legs he has!

I can see his eyes,
Small and black and shiny.
I can't think how it feels to be so tiny!

Rhoda W. Bacmeister

Fuzzy Wuzzy, Creepy Crawly

Fuzzy wuzzy, creepy crawly
     Caterpillar funny,
You will be a butterfly
     When the days are sunny.

Winging, flinging, dancing, springing
     Butterfly so yellow,
You were once a caterpillar,
     Wiggly, wiggly fellow.

Lillian Schulz

The Ducks

When our ducks waddle to the pond,
They're awkward as awkward can be.
But when they get in the water and swim,
They glide most gracefully.

Alice Wilkins

The Squirrel

Whisky, frisky,
Hippity hop;
Up he goes
To the tree top!

Whirly, twirly,
Round and round,
Down he scampers
To the ground.

Furly, curly,
What a tail!
Tall as a feather
Broad as a sail!

Where's his supper?
In the shell,
Snappity, crackity,
Out it fell.

Anonymous

Birthday Cake

If little mice have birthdays
(and I suppose they do)

And have a family party
(and guests invited too)

And have a cake with candles
(it would be rather small)

I bet a birthday CHEESE cake
would please them most of all.

Aileen Fisher

The Cold Old House

I know a house, and a cold old house,
    A cold old house by the sea.
If I were a mouse in that cold old house
    What a cold cold mouse I'd be!

Anonymous

At The Seaside

When I was down beside the sea
A wooden spade they gave to me
> To dig the sandy shore.
My holes were empty like a cup,
In every hole the sea came up,
> Till it could come no more.

Robert Louis Stevenson

I'm Glad

I'm glad the sky is painted blue,
And the earth is painted green,
With such a lot of nice fresh air
All sandwiched in between.

Anonymous

A Kite

I often sit and wish that I
Could be a kite up in the sky,
And ride upon the breeze and go
Whichever way I chanced to blow.

Anonymous

Rain

Rain on the green grass,
  And rain on the tree,
And rain on the house-top,
  But not upon me!

Anonymous

Little Wind

Little wind, blow on the hilltop,
Little wind, blow on the plain;
Little wind, blow up the sunshine,
Little wind, blow off the rain.

Kate Greenaway

My Zipper Suit

My zipper suit is bunny brown—
The top zips up, the legs zip down.
I wear it every day.
My daddy brought it out from town.
Zip it up, and zip it down,
And hurry out to play!

Marie Louise Allen

First Snow

Snow makes whiteness where it falls.
The bushes look like popcorn-balls.
And places where I always play,
Look like somewhere else today.

Marie Louise Allen

The Park

I'm glad that I
     Live near a park

For in the winter
     After dark

The park lights shine
     As bright and still

As dandelions
     On a hill.

James S. Tippett

Firefly

A little light is going by,
Is going up to see the sky,
A little light with wings.

I never could have thought of it,
To have a little bug all lit
And made to go on wings.

Elizabeth Madox Roberts

Silly Puppy

Although he hates
To have his bath,
He seems to think
It's fun
To dip his paws
Into the tub,
When I am
Having one.

Kathryn Jackson

Hippity Hop To Bed

O it's hippity hop to bed!
I'd rather sit up instead.
But when father says "must,"
There's nothing but just
Go hippity hop to bed.

Leroy F. Jackson